Coloring test page

STARFISH

NARWHAL

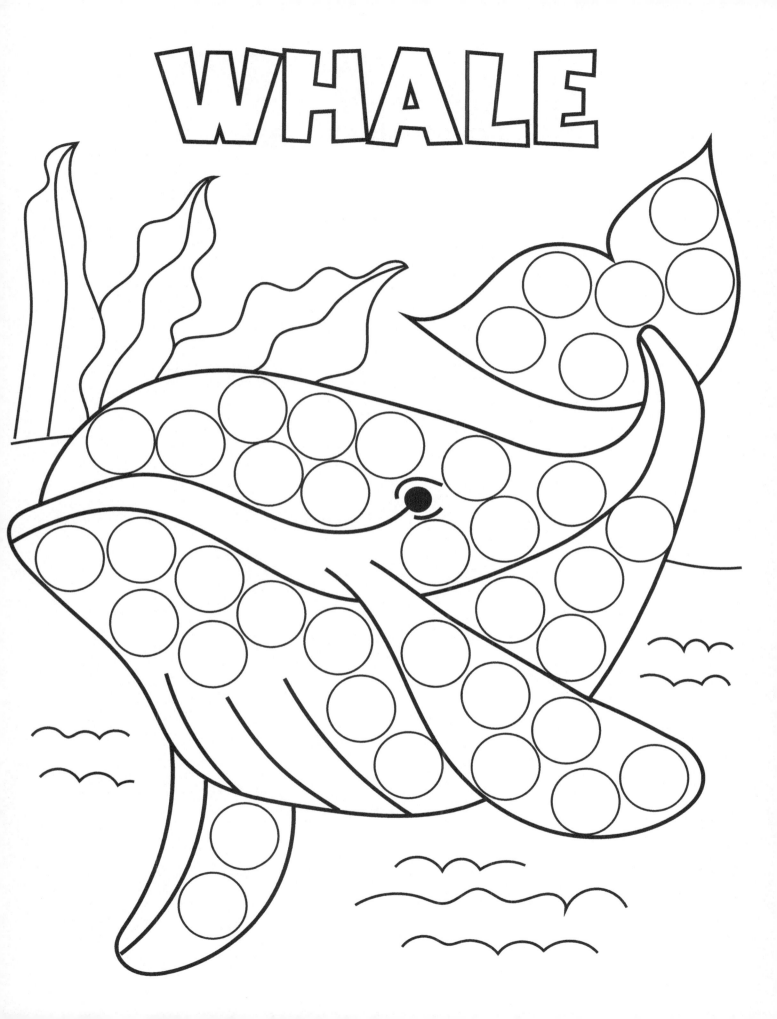

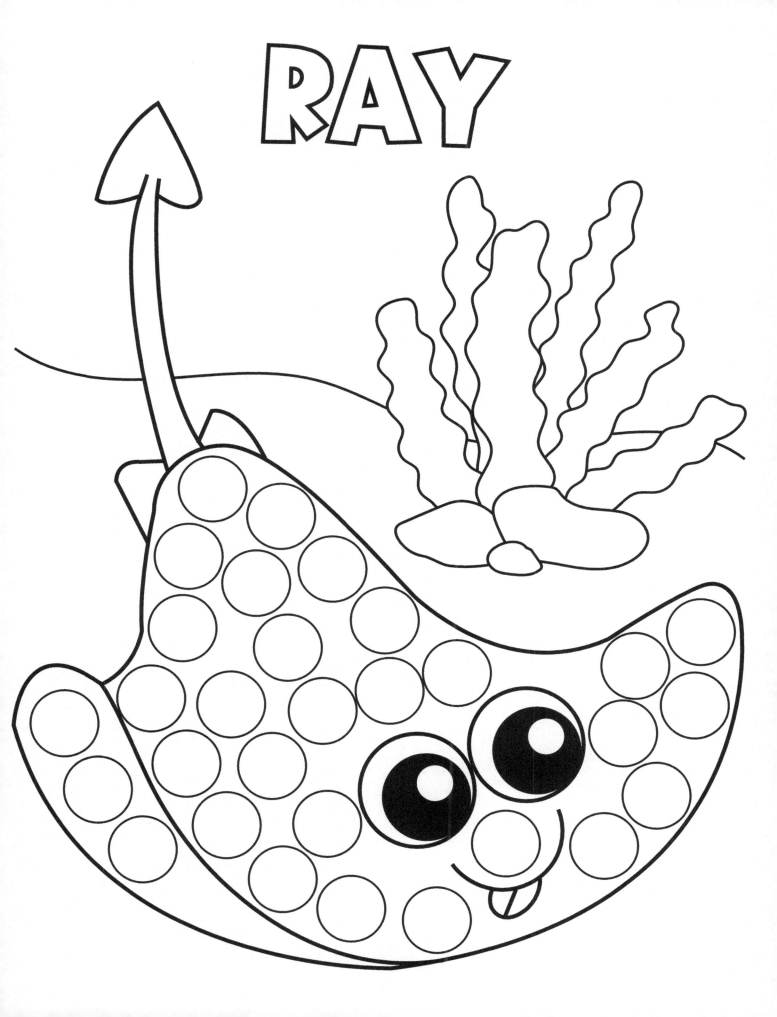

SEAHORSE

ANGLERFISH

SEAL

LOBSTER

JELLYFISH

BLUE WHALE

HERMIT CRAB

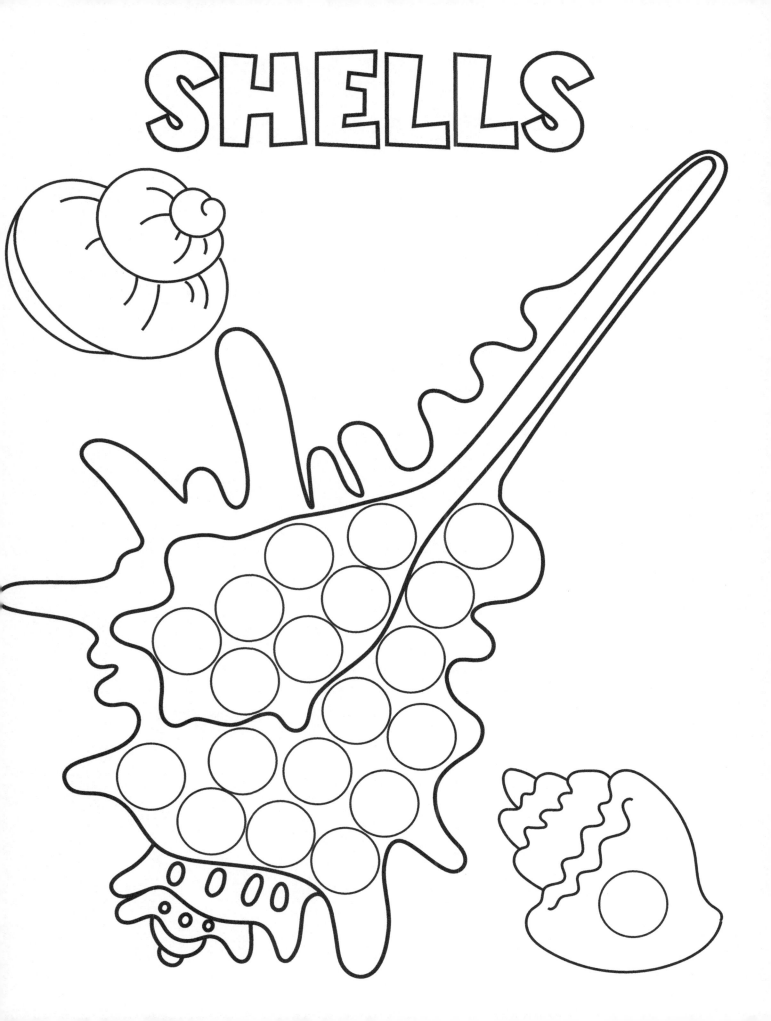

MOSASAURUS

MOORISH IDOL

DOLPHIN

PUFFER

SHRIMP

ANEMONE

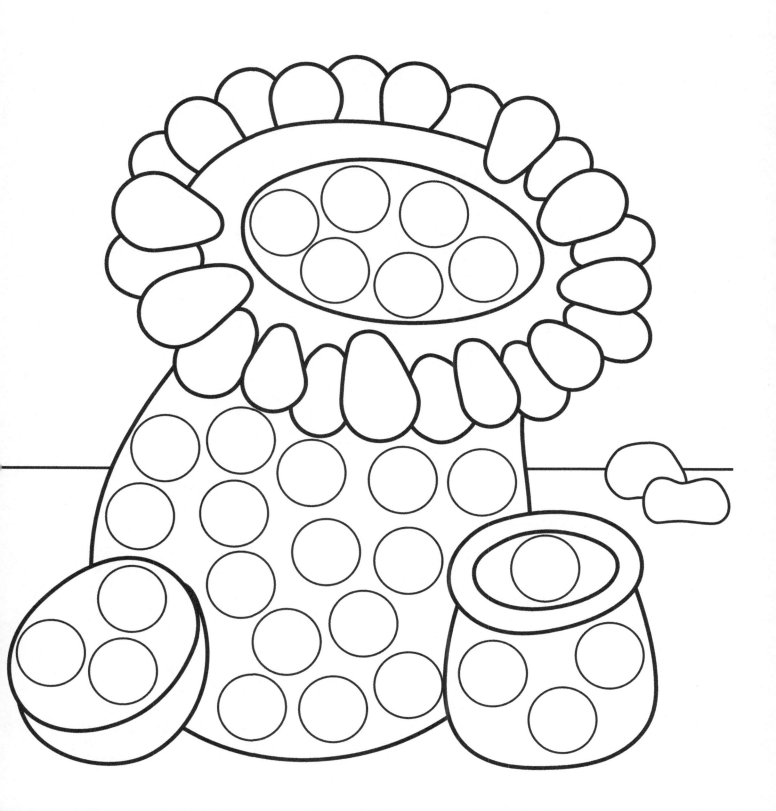

MANATEE

PLESIOSAUR

SWORDFISH

TROPICAL FISH

KILLER WHALE

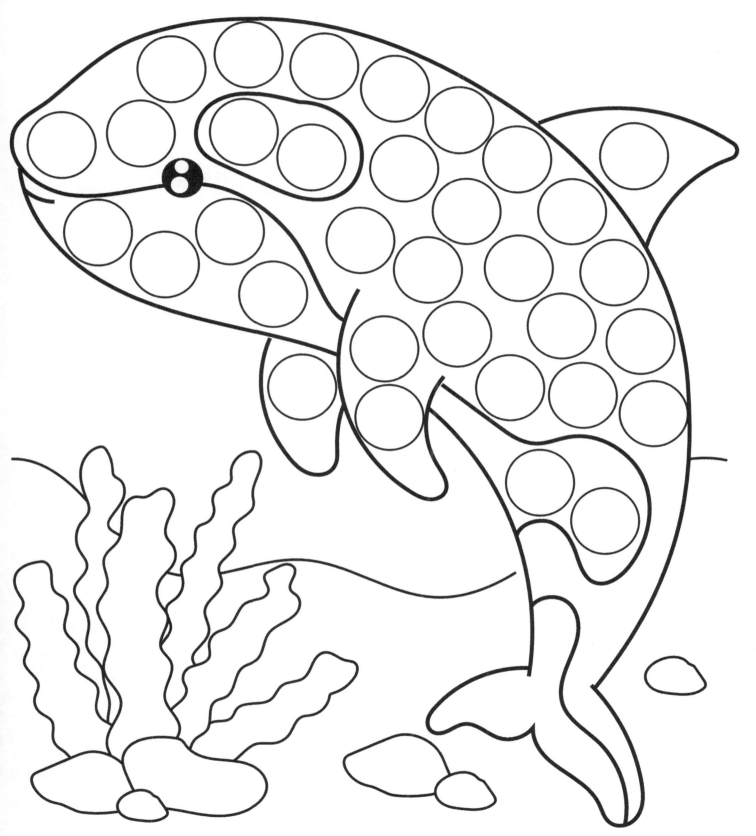

PLATYPUS

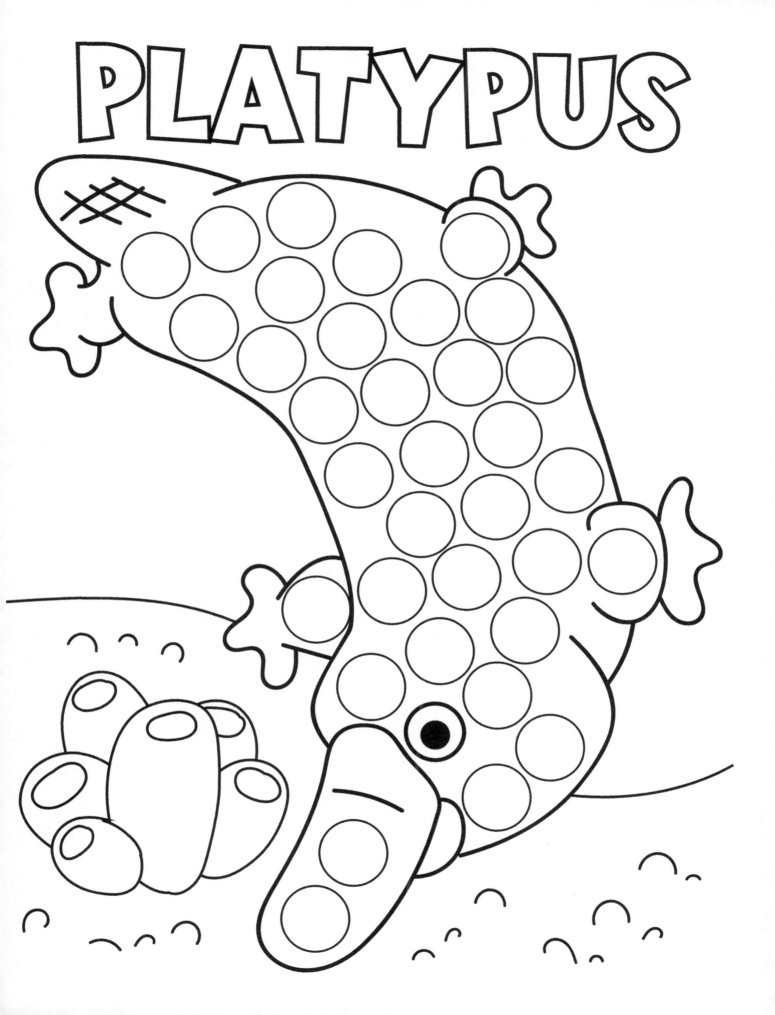

WHALE SHARK

SAWFISH

ANGEL SHARK

LEOPARD SHARK

HAMMER SHARK

SPERM WHALE

MANTA RAY

SEI WHALE

FIN WHALE

BELUGA WHALE

GREY WHALE

SEA SLUG

CORAL

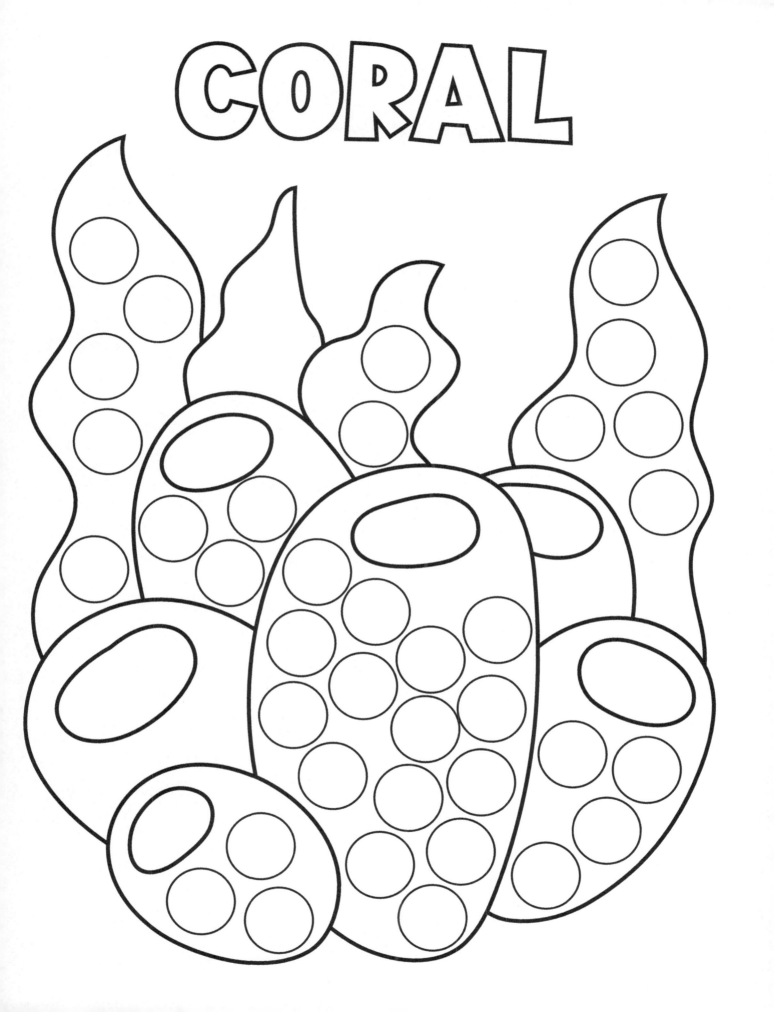

PENGUIN

SEA URCHIN

WALRUS

FLYING FISH

SEA CUCUMBER

Made in the USA
Las Vegas, NV
27 November 2023

81692109R00059